Lil Mondo Travel Challenge Books are inspired by real people and real places. We hope they engage your children in the cultures, history, food and language of the places they're lucky enough to visit.

Lil Mondo's challenges are best suited for ages 5 to 12, and we find it best to score the challenges on the level of effort.

From our family to yours, travel happy!

Check out www.lilmondo.com for our latest destinations

A BRAVE BIRD DESIGN
www.bravebird.com.au

LET'S MAKE SURE EVERYONE KNOWS THIS BOOK IS YOURS!

THIS BELONGS TO

MY NAME IS ....

I AM .... YEARS OLD.

I AM FROM THE COUNTRY OF ....

WHEN IT'S 9:00AM AT HOME, IT IS .... IN JAPAN.

IN JAPAN ONE .... OF MY MONEY AT HOME EQUALS

.... JAPANESE YEN.

The perfect time to fill this out is on the plane going to Japan.

HI THERE, I'M **LIL MONDO** AND I'VE GOT A LITTLE SECRET...

DRAW A LINE ON THE MAP SHOWING ME HOW YOU WILL GET FROM YOUR HOME COUNTRY to JAPAN.

So here's how we play the game

I've got 6 topics to help you explore Japan, and each topic has 3 challenges: easy (10 points), medium (20 points) and hard (30 points).

That's 18 incredible challenges altogether!

You can do these challenges in any order you want.

There is no 'right' or 'wrong' answer.

Your grown-ups will give you a score on how much effort you put in, and you can keep track on the scoreboard on the next page.

YOU'RE TOTALLY GOING TO LOVE JAPAN!

SCOREBOARD

Manga Madness	/10	/20	/30
The Way of the Gods	/10	/20	/30
Just Rice? Think twice!	/10	/20	/30
Traditions of Japan	/10	/20	/30
Techno-Titans	/10	/20	/30
Terrific Tokyo!	/10	/20	/30

MANGA MADNESS

"Manga" is the name for Japanese comics - and they are not just for kids! Japanese love their Manga characters - they make up stories about where they come from, what they like, what they hate - even what they eat.

DID YOU KNOW? Manga comes from 'man' and 'ga' and means crazy sketches. 1 out of every 4 books sold in Japan is a Manga comic.

HERE ARE SOME OF THE MOST POPULAR MANGA CHARACTERS

AstroBoy is a robot who uses his superior powers to fight crime and can feel human emotions.

Doraemon is a robot cat who travels back in time to help a young schoolboy with his life.

Goku explores his world searching for "dragonballs" that command a magical dragon.

Find me at least one of these Manga Superheroes as you walk around - and take a photo.

10 POINTS

tick this box when you're done! ⟶ ☐

With one of your grown ups, go up to a local, see if they speak English and then ASK THEM these three questions.

What is your favourite Manga character?

....

....

....

Why is this your favourite Manga character?

....

....

....

Write your Manga character's name in Japanese:

30 POINTS

Draw your own Manga superhero with a twist - your hero has to always carry a pot plant. Weird, I know.

DRAW IN THIS SPACE

My Superhero's name is ....

....

My Superhero is super because ....

....

....

WAY OF THE GODS

"Shinto" is a religion practiced mainly in Japan, and it means "way of the Gods. Shinto followers believe that spirits called "kami" live inside everyday things - from rocks, to mountains, to trees. Many Japanese visit Shinto Shrines where they try to make the 'kami' spirits happy - which brings them good luck!

DID YOU KNOW? Shinto Shrines and Buddhist Temples look very different from the outside. Colour in these pictures and learn how to spot the difference. It will definitely impress your grown-ups!

SHINTO SHRINES

BUDDHIST TEMPLE

COLOUR ME IN

Japanese people do interesting stuff when they visit shrines and temples. When you visit one, watch carefully and write down three things that they do.

10 POINTS

1. ....

2. ....

3. ....

20 POINTS

Can you find the words in the puzzle?

Words are hidden → and ↓

COLOUR ME IN

```
G A A K Q V C Z L R G
S H R I N E T O R I I
T P N M K C K A M I U
E R S H I N T O M Z P
M I W L N D K W T H J
P E G L Q N K R H C E
L S B U D D H A Z Z E
E T Y L Z L G N D K M
F X O W J S D X B D T
```

BUDDHA

KAMI

PRIEST

SHINTO

SHRINE

TEMPLE

TORII

 30 POINTS — When you're at a Shinto Shrine, find out what a "Torii" is - and draw one by connecting the dots.

A TORII IS:

_____

_____

JUST RICE? THINK TWICE!

Many travellers say eating in Japan is one of the best parts of their trip. Traditional foods include everything from pancakes to soups to eating raw fish!!! Japanese take table manners very seriously. But slurping your noodles is a polite way of showing how much you love the taste!

DID YOU KNOW? When eating, Japanese people say Itadakimasu, which means "I receive this food" - a nice way of saying thank you to the cook.

Find out how to say these three things in Japanese and write down how the word sounds in English:

CHOPSTICKS _____

TEA _____

RICE _____

COLOUR ME IN

IMPRESS YOUR PARENTS BY USING THESE WORDS

breakfast	=	asa gohan
lunch	=	ranchi
dinner	=	dina
snack	=	sunak-ku
chicken	=	tori-niku
fish	=	sakana
pork	=	buta-niku

Time for a sweet challenge! Try at least two different kinds of desserts, then draw what they look like and describe the taste.

20 POINTS

DRAW IN THESE SPACES ↘

TASTES LIKE:
....
....
....

TASTES LIKE:
....
....
....

Here are 4 totally different types of Japanese food.

You have to try them ALL and write down how they taste, and score them out of 5.

30 POINTS

MISO
___ /5
....
....
....

RAMEN
___ /5
....
....
....

YAKITORI
___ /5
....
....
....

SOBA NOODLES
___ /5
....
....
....

TRADITIONS OF JAPAN

Japan has a history going back thousands of years, and many of their traditions are not found anywhere else in the world. Don't forget to enjoy the unique sounds of Japanese culture - Geishas giggling, Sumos Stomping or Business people bowing!

DID YOU KNOW? Sumo Wrestling started more than 1500 years ago as a way to pray for a good rice season. Wrestlers, known as Rikishi, eat 10 times what a normal adult would eat!

What do you think would be in a Rikishi's pantry? Fill in the gaps above.

HERE IS A CLUE:

They eat loads of healthy stuff - not junk food!

10 POINTS

DRAW IN THIS SPACE

DID YOU KNOW?

Japan has an ancient tradition of artistic writing called "Shodo". Many letters look like the words they describe - like this one 山 which means "mountain".

日本

20 POINTS — Try to copy exactly these letters for "Nihon" (which means Japan in Japanese).

DRAW IN THIS SPACE

DID YOU KNOW?

Japan has a unique type of poetry, called "Haiku". It has VERY strict rules. It is always three lines long - with 7 syllables (sounds in a word) in the first line, 5 syllables in the middle line, and 7 syllables in the last line.

Here is an example - you can count the syllables to check:

I-am-first-with-five
Then-sev-en-in-the-mid-dle
Five-ag-ain-to-end

 30 POINTS Write a Haiku about what it's like to visit Japan.

WRITE YOUR HAIKU HERE

TECHNO TITANS

Japan is a world leader in coming up with great inventions and new technologies. Some of the biggest technology companies in the world call Japan home.

DID YOU KNOW? Japan invented the bullet train. Make sure you get to the train station on time. The average delay for Japanese bullet trains is only 36 seconds!

STICK YOUR BULLET TRAIN TICKET HERE

WHY DID tHE JAPANESE ROBOt CROSS tHE ROAD?

20 POINTS

Write down a funny answer and test the joke on someone. You only get the 20 points if you make someone laugh!

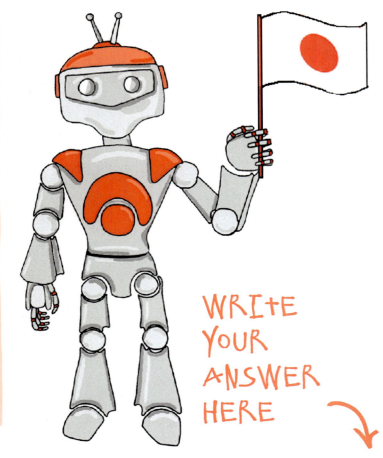

WRItE YOUR ANSWER HERE ↓

Come up with a crazy invention that links two of Japan's greatest inventions – the wristwatch and 2-minute noodles.

DRAW IN THIS SPACE

TERRIFIC TOKYO

Tokyo is big! 39 million people live in Greater Tokyo - officially the biggest population of any city in the world! Tokyo is also tiny! It is famous for hotels where people curl up inside tiny capsules for the night.

DID YOU KNOW? Tokyo has the busiest road crossing in the world, called Shibuya. Try to get there and count the people crossing at once.

DID YOU KNOW?

Tokyo Tower can be seen from many parts of the city. It was actually inspired by the Eiffel Tower in Paris.

 10 POINTS — Take TWO selfies with the Tokyo Tower from two totally different parts of the city.

tICK tHIS BOX WHEN YOU'RE DONE!

 BONUS POINTS — Cut out the mask towards the back and get creative with your posing!

DID YOU KNOW?

Tokyo loves weird stuff! Ever wanted a coffee with 20 cats? Or a restaurant where rabbits bring your food? How about waiters dressed up as Manga characters serving Manga food?

 Draw your perfect Weird Tokyo Cafe - and give the cafe a name!

DRAW IN THIS SPACE

YOUR CAFE IS CALLED: _____

30 POINTS Write a postcard to someone who lived in Tokyo 100 years ago. Tell them what their city is like as you see it today. Describe the sights, sounds, smells and tastes in front of you.

Tokyo just 100 years ago

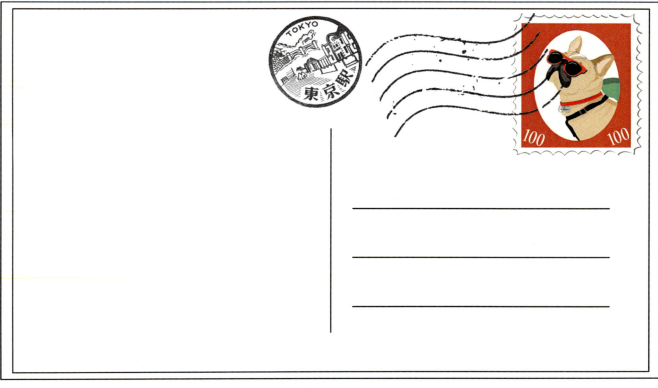

WELL, THAT'S IT!

We've come to the end of our challenges for the beautiful country of Japan.

Together we saw how amazing Japan is, from its delicious food to new technologies that have changed the world.

As you've worked through the challenges, I hope you scored some great rewards from your grown-ups along the way.

You should totally keep this Travel Challenge Book as a souvenir of your trip to Japan. Until our next awesome destination together.

SAYONARA!

LIL MONDO

So now you're an experienced Japan traveller! What will you tell your friends are the three VERY best things to do in Japan?

What are the funniest or most amazing moments from this trip that you'll want to remember as an adult? Try and list at least 3.

Make a list of the things you miss the most about being away from home?

CUT OUT THIS MASK AND GET CREATIVE WITH YOUR HOLIDAY SNAPS!